TAOISM

First Edition 2002

Taoism

ISBN 7-119-03061-2

© Foreign Languages Press
Published by Foreign Languages Press
24 Baiwanzhuang Road, Beijing 100037, China
Home Page: http://www.flp.com.cn
E-mail Addresses: info@flp.com.cn
sales@flp.com.cn
Distributed by China International Book Trading Corporation
35 Chegongzhuang Xilu, Beijing 100044, China
P.O. Box 399, Beijing, China

Printed in the People's Republic of China

TAOISM

By the Taoist Association of China

Foreign Languages Press   Beijing

Contents

Preface   6

A General Introduction to Taoism in China   7

I. The Beliefs of Taoism, and Its Deities and Immortals   12

II. Taoist Priests, Taoist Rituals, and the Life of Taoists   30

III. Taoist Musical Instruments and Ritual Articles   54

IV. Taoist *Gongfu* and Alchemy   70

V. Sacred Mountains, Taoist Palaces and Temples   78

Appendixes

i. Sketch Map of Sacred Taoist Mountains,
   Palaces and Temples in China

ii. Main Taoist Festivals and Grand Ceremonies

Preface

Taoism regards Tao, or the Way, as its ultimate belief. The "Tao" that we believe in is fundamentally the "void" or nothingness yet encompassing everything. Therefore, we always advocate the spirit of tolerance. In this world exist many cultures and religions, large in number and distinct in nature. We believe that these distinctions do not necessarily lead to conflict. Taoism advocates the Tao's way in accordance with the law of Nature. Although Nature may be composed of very different species, it goes on in a harmonious and systematic way. As long as we can tolerate each other and respect each other's beliefs, values and lifestyles, we will be able to live in harmony with each other.

To cultivate in people a sense of tolerance and harmony, Taoism advocates the spirit of "universal love." "Universal love" is to maintain a benevolent loving heart towards all people, be their family members or strangers, the great or the humble. Taoism calls for people to feel happy about the wellbeing of others, sympathize with others in suffering, help those in danger, support those in need, and feel joyous over others' gains and sorrowful for their losses just as we do over our own gains and losses. If every one of us cherish a loving heart, is there any conflict in the world that cannot be resolved?

Today, the Taoist Association of China, at the request of the Foreign Languages Press, has compiled this album of *Taoism* for people overseas. This is a worthwhile endeavor to spread Taoist culture and promote exchange and dialogue between Taoism and other cultures and religions in the world. I am honored to write the preface for such an album.

Min Zhiting
Director of the Taoist Association of China

A General Introduction to Taoism in China

Taoism is an indigenous traditional religion of China. It is generally believed that Taoist organizations were formally established 1,900 years ago by Celestial Master Zhang Daoling during the reign (AD 126-144) of Emperor Shundi of the Eastern Han Dynasty. However, the original sources of Taoist doctrines can be traced back to the Spring and Autumn Period and the Warring States Period (770-221 BC). Thus there is the common reference to the "Three Ancestors" that alludes to the Yellow Emperor, Lao Zi and Celestial Master Zhang.

The ideological system of Taoism covers a wide range of contents. Generally speaking, it evolved into a religious culture by basing itself on ancient religious beliefs in China around the worship of heaven and ancestors, as well as Taoist theories and beliefs regarding immortality arising during the Spring and Autumn Period and the Warring States Period. It has also absorbed ethical ideas from Confucianism and folk religious customs.

The core of Taoism is, of course, Tao (the Way), which is beyond description. It is said that Tao is the origin of the universe,the basis of all existing things, the law governing their development and change, and the ultimate god of Taoism. The concept of Virtue (De) is closely related to Tao. *Dao De Jing* relates, "All respect Tao yet value Virtue." Virtue has different connotations. One common explanation is that Virtue is the specific manifestation of Tao in specific things.

Taoists regard Tao and Virtue as the general principles of their beliefs and behavior. They should not only cultivate Tao but also accumulate Virtue. Therefore, both Tao and Virtue serve as the basis of Taoist doctrines. Derived from the foundation of Tao and Virtue are a whole set of principles, including nonaction, non-passion and non-desire, non-struggle, and the pursuit of simplicity and truth.

Taoists believe in both Tao as well as in deities and immortals. "Gods" in Taoism refer to the Celestial Worthy of Primordial Beginning, the Celestial Worthy of Numinous Treasure and the Celestial Worthy of the Way and Its Virtue, the Jade Emperor and the Great Emperor of Zhenwu, who were born before heaven and earth separated; while "immortals" refer to humans who were born after heaven and earth separated and transformed into deities, becoming immortals through cultivating Tao. Among them are Celestial Master Zhang and Lü Chunyang. From the Taoist perspective, both gods and immortals are symbols of Tao. There exists a hierarchy of gods and immortals in Taoism. At the top of the hierarchy are the gods of the highest ranks   the Celestial   Worthy of Primordial Beginning, the Celestial Worthy of Numinous Treasure and the Celestial Worthy of the Way and Its Virtue, who are the embodiment of Tao or may be said to be the Tao itself. Below them are the gods of the lower ranks, who are entrusted with responsibilities according to their attainments in Tao and Virtue. The highest among them is the Jade Emperor, followed by the four major deities and other celestial beings. The Jade Emperor is the highest ruler of the universe. Different deities and immortals have different responsibilities. Among the most popularly known are the celestial beings in charge of wind, rain, thunder, lightning, water and fire, the God of Wealth, the Kitchen God, the God of the Town and the God of the Land.

Taoism believes that the universe contains 36 heavens above and 36 hells below. The highest heaven is called Ta-luo Heaven. The next three heavens are the Realm of Absolute Purity; the four heavens after that are the Four Brahmas; while the rest of the 28 heavens include the Immaterial Realm (four heavens), the Material Realm (18 heavens), and the Realm of Desire (six heavens).

Ta-luo Heaven is wherein dwells the Celestial Worthy of Primordial Beginning, the Celestial Worthy of Numinous Treasure and the Celestial Worthy of the Way and Its Virtue; the Realm of Absolute Purity is the abode of nine grades of saints, realized beings and immortals. Those in the Four Brahmas are free of the pain of life and death; those in the Immaterial Realm enjoy longevity but are not free from the pain of life and death; while the people in the Realm of Desire experience all manner of desire as well as pain.

The 36 hells are the netherworld where the souls of the deceased dwell. Taoism believes that the deceased will be judged by the Ten Kings of the netherworld. A benevolent person will be reincarnated, while an evil-doer will be subject to punishment in these hells.

Taoism also believes that, among the famous mountains of the earth, there are 10 Big Taoist Caves, 36 Small Taoist Caves and 72 Promised Lands, which serve as the abodes of immortals. Among the four seas, there are 10 continents and three islands, where immortals take rest and the divine grass grows. It is believed that if one eats this grass, one will become immortal. In Chinese history, the First Emperor of the Qin Dynasty and Emperor Wudi of the Han Dynasty sent people to look for these fairy islands off the sea in hopes of obtaining those elixirs.

The highest ideal of a Taoist is to acquire immortality. To achieve this goal, one must practice Taoism both inside and outside one's physical existence. Inner practice involves physical and breathing exercises, concentrated contemplation, and the taking of elixirs. Later, this type of practice gradually came down to refining the interior elixirs (*neidan*). The basic principle of this practice is still to cultivate the self both spiritually and physically. External practice involves doing good deeds and helping others so as to acquire more merit and virtue. If one succeeds in both aspects, one could enter the world of immortals.

The books that record Taoist doctrines are referred to as the Taoist scriptures. There were different kinds of Taoist scriptures compiled at different moments in history, all under the title of the *Taoist Canon*. The earliest *Taoist Canon* appeared during the Tang Dynasty, followed by other editions compiled during the Song, Jin, Yuan and Ming dynasties. Extant today are two editions respectively compiled during the reign of Zhengtong and the reign of Wangli of the Ming Dynasty, hence the names: *Zhengtong Taoist Canon* and *Wanli Supplementary Taoist Canon*. The decree from a Yuan-dynasty emperor to burn *Taoist Canon* resulted in the loss of a great number of Taoist doctrines. Today, the Taoist Association of China is making efforts to recompile an anthology of Taoist doctrines, entitled *China's Taoist Canon*.

The *Dao De Jing* by Lao Zi is Taoism's principal and most important canon. Other canons include *Book of Secret Revelations*, *Book of Purity and Quietness*, *Book of the Lower Elixir Field*, *Book of Divine*

Deliverance, and *Can Tong Qi*.

Many schools of Taoism were formed throughout history. During the Han Dynasty, there arose Tianshi Taoism and Taiping Taoism; during the Wei and Jin Period, there were the Shangqing Sect, the Lingbao Sect, and the Sanhuang Sect; the Song, Jin and Yuan dynasties saw Quanzhen Taoism, Taiyi Taoism, Zhenda Taoism, and Jinming Taoism. Historical fusion brought many different sects together, from which two important sects, the Zhengyi Sect (evolved from Tianshi Taoism) and Quanzhen Taoism (founded by Wang Chongyang), finally developed. Today's Taoist followers belong to either of these two sects. The Zhengyi Sect is popular mainly in Jiangxi, Jiangsu, Shanghai and Fujian provinces, while Quanzhen Taoism flourishes in other parts of China. There is no difference in basic beliefs between the two sects, with the only differences lying in their norms and regulations. Quanzhen Taoism, for example, requires its followers to be vegetarians, remain single and live in temples, while the Zhengyi Sect has no such regulations at all.

Sites for Taoist activities are called Taoist Palaces *(gong)* or temples *(guan)*. Taoists in the early days preferred to build their temples in wild but serene mountains and forests. With the spread of Taoism, more and more temples were built in urban areas. Each of them came to enshrine a great number of statues of deities and immortals. Taoists lived in the temples, practicing Tao and conducting sacred rites. Ordinary believers frequented these places to burn joss sticks and worship the gods. These temples were open to visitors, too. On the birthdays of the main gods and immortals, grand services were held in the temples, attracting a steady flow of people who came to offer incense sticks and to pray for blessings. Some temples also sponsored fairs, which brought together the worship of gods with recreational and trading activities, to produce lively festivities.

Taoism, during its time-honored history of development, has exerted far-reaching influences on China's philosophy, literature, arts, medicine and science. What merits special attention is its great contribution to ancient Chinese medicine and chemistry. A folk saying goes, "Nine out of 10 Taoists are doctors." Taoists' pursuit of longevity and health resulted in many Taoists excelling in medicine. Some renowned senior Taoists, like Ge Hong of the Jin Dynasty, Tao Hongjing of the Southern and Northern Dynasties and Sun

Simiao of the Tang Dynasty, were all well-known doctors and pharmacists. Taoists of early times attached great importance to minerals, mainly lead, mercury, sulfur, gold, and silver, from which they believed elixirs could be made. They had hoped that these elixirs could free them from the terrors of death. Of course, no immortality pills were ever achieved, but during this process they discovered certain chemical phenomena, which they recorded. Their records thus became the most valuable documents in ancient Chinese chemistry. Joseph Needham, historian of science, wrote in his *Science and Civilization in China*: "Many of the most attractive elements of the Chinese character derive from Taoism. China without Taoism would be a tree of which some of its deepest roots had perished." What is worth mentioning here is that gunpowder, one of China's four great inventions, was actually invented by Taoists during their attempts to create elixirs.

Taoist culture has long permeated the everyday life of ordinary Chinese people since it exerted great influences on social customs in ancient China and on the shaping of national consciousness. The venerated Lu Xun, the great Chinese writer, once said, "China is rooted in Taoism." Taoism has played an important role in the making of traditional Chinese culture. To know it is to possess a key to a better understanding of traditional Chinese culture.

Today, as one of the five major religions (Taoism, Buddhism, Islam, Protestantism, and Roman Catholicism) in China, Taoism has a great number of followers. There are more than 1,600 temples and more than 25,000 Taoist priests of the Quanzhen Taoism and the Zhengyi Sect. The number of ordinary believers is almost impossible to assess.

Taoism has also found its way to other parts of the world. Taoist methods of keeping fit and healthy, as well as the Taoist concept of harmonious coexistence between humans and nature, have claimed a great deal of attention. Taoism is attracting the interest of an increasing number of people worldwide.

The emblem of Taoism is the Taiji symbol, or diagram of the cosmological scheme, comprised of a circle with an S-shaped line dividing the white *(yang)* and black *(yin)* halves.

I. The Beliefs of Taoism, and Its Deities and Immortals

The supreme belief of Taoism is "Tao" ('the Way'), which is indescribable and beyond human perception and understanding. "Tao" is believed to be the origin of the universe, the basis of the existence of all creatures, and the laws of development and change ruling all creatures. "Tao" sublimates into the *qi* (vital energy or breath), and gathers to form the Three Purities, i.e., the Celestial Worthy of Primordial Beginning or Jade Purity, the Celestial Worthy of Numinous Treasure or Highest Purity, and the Celestial Worthy of the Way and Its Virtue or Supreme Purity. Below the Three Purities, the emanations of Tao, are a mass of deities such as the Jade Emperor, the Four Heavenly Emperors and the Five Emperors of the Five Directions, and the immortals who humans can become through self-cultivation. Deities and immortals, models in achieving Tao, make it their duty to teach and redeem all creatures, and are therefore worshiped by the Taoism followers.

A painting of Lao Zi. ▶

Lao Zi.
According to Taoism, Lao Zi was the incarnation of Supreme Purity. It is said that he was once a historiographer of the Zhou Dynasty (c.1100-221 BC), who resigned his post to journey westward when he saw that the dynasty was in decline. At Hangu Pass, Yin Xi, the commander of the pass, aware that he was a sage, asked him to write a book to teach the "Tao". Lao Zi wrote a two-volume book, known to later generations as *Dao De Jing (Canon of the Tao and Its Virtue)*. The book is the foremost Taoist scripture, with Lao Zi being recognized as the originator of Taoism.

A stele depicting Lao Zi. ▶
This image of Lao Zi was from a painting by Wu Daozi, a famous Tang-dynasty artist. The stele bears praise to Lao Zi, written by the Emperor Xuanzong and the great calligrapher Yan Zhenqing of the Tang Dynasty (AD 618-907). The stele was carved during the Song Dynasty (AD 960-1279).

A statue of Lao Zi, in Quanzhou, Fujian Province, carved during the Song Dynasty.

The Celestial Worthy of Numinous Treasure

The Celestial Worthy of Primordial Beginning

The Celestial Worthy of the Way and Its Virtue

The Three Purities.

The Three Purities were the supreme Taoist deities: the Celestial Worthy of Primordial Beginning, the Celestial Worthy of Numinous Treasure, and the Celestial Worthy of the Way and Its Virtue. They rule over the highest three celestial realms of Jade Purity, Highest Purity, and Great Purity. According to Taoism, they are emanations of Tao, omnipresent and supreme.

Jade Emperor.
The Jade Emperor is believed to be the highest deity ruling the universe, lower only to the Three Purities, parallel to the emperor in the human world.

Taoist Divinities in Pilgrimage.
Taoism is polytheism. Its deities include divinities in heaven, the gods of mountains, rivers and land, and immortals. This painting shows a section of a scene of Taoist divinities having an audience with the Jade Emperor.

Birthday celebration for the Queen
Mother of the West.
The Queen Mother of the West is
believed to be the highest goddess in
Taoism. On her birthday, which is said
to be on the third day of the third lunar
month, all divinities and immortals come
to her Feast of Peaches for a celebration.

Gouchen,a celestial emperor representing the constellation surrounding the Polar Star

Ziwei, Emperor of the North Polar Star

Great Emperor of Longevity of the South Polar Star

Houtu, the Earth Goddess

The Four Heavenly Emperors.
The Four Heavenly Emperors are Gouchen, a celestial emperor representing the constellation surrounding the Polar Star; Ziwei, Emperor of the North Polar Star; the Great Emperor of Longevity of the South Polar Star; and Houtu, the Earth Goddess. They assist Jade Emperor in ruling the universe.

The Three Divine Officials on a Tour of Inspection.
The three divine officials are the Official of Heaven, the Official of Earth, and the Official of Water. It is said that the Official of Heaven bestows blessings, the Official of Earth pardons sins, and the Official of Water eliminates disasters. They make tours to inspect good and evil, and to protect all creatures.

The Great Emperor Zhenwu, the Perfected Warrior.
A heavenly god of the northern hemisphere. Ancient Chinese civilization harmonized the four directions with four spiritual beings. The tortoise and snake, corresponding with the north, were the symbol of the Great Emperor Zhenwu.

A bronze statue of Xuanwu (or Zhenwu, a tortoise entwined by a snake) on Mount Wudang. ▶

The Taoist God of Mercy.
A heavenly god believed to deliver people from all manner of troubles and sufferings. It is said that he answers to prayers or to the calling of his name.

A relief of the three star-gods of Happiness, Rank and Affluence and Longevity.

The Three Star-gods of Happiness, Rank and Affluence, and Longevity. The triad is composed of the three Taoist gods Tianguan, Wenchang and Shouxing. Tianguan bestows blessings, Wenchang grants official titles, and Shouxing grants years of life. They are popular gods among the common Chinese people.

The Old Man of the Southern Celestial Pole. The Old Man of the Southern Celestial Pole, also known as Shouxing, is a symbol of long life. He is highly celebrated among the common Chinese people.

The God of the Town and the God of the Land.
The God of the Town is the guardian of towns and cities, while the God of the Land is the guardian of villages. In Taoist rituals, Taoist priests invite deities through the God of the Town, and send them off through the God of the Land.

The God of the Land   The God of the Town

Xie Bi'an and Fan Wujiu.
These two marshals under the God of the Town are escorting criminals.

Xie Bi'an   Fan Wujiu.

The Four Immortals Celebrating a Birthday. This Ming-dynasty painting portrays the refined demeanor of the four immortals.

A relief of the Eight Immortals crossing the sea. The Eight Immortals are: Zhongli Quan, Lü Dongbin, Zhang Guolao, Cao Guojiu, Li Tieguai, Han Xiangzi, Lan Caihe, and He Xiangu. They are models of achieving immortality through self-cultivation.

Riding the Dragon.
The dragon is a divine creature worshiped by Taoists. This painting, dating back to the Southern Song Dynasty, presents a scene of someone achieving immortality and ascending to Heaven.

Immortals.
Accentuating life and abhorring death, Taoism believes that through persistent self-cultivation one can achieve immortality. The four immortals depicted in this painting vary in age, which shows their different levels of achievement of the Tao.

Celestial Master Zhang.
Celestial Master Zhang, or Zhang Daoling, is one of the founders of Taoist religion.

Perfect man (Zhenren) Qiu Changchun on His Travels.
Perfect man Changchun, also known as Qiu Chuji, is the founder of the
Longmen Group of the Quanzhen Sect of Taoism. During the chaos of
war at the end of the Jin Dynasty and the beginning of the Yuan Dynasty,
he traveled a long way to the Western Regions to visit Genghis Khan,
admonishing him against killing innocent people.

II. Taoist Priests, Taoist Rituals, and the Life of Taoists

Taoist priests gather together for morning and evening prayers each day. They hold prayer rituals to give blessings on the birthdays of deities or on festivals, and conduct rituals to expiate the sins of the dead on the Festival of Pure Brightness and the Festival of Spirits of the Dead. Such rituals can also be held at the request of followers. Unveiling ceremonies are held when a monastery is completed. Taoist priests also hold large-scale rituals, such as the Grand Universe Ceremony, to pray for prosperity and peace in the nation, good weather for crops, and world peace. Besides conducting rituals, Taoist priests are mainly engaged in self-cultivation.

The Abbot Wang Changyue of the White Cloud
Temple in the early years of the Qing Dynasty.

Taoist priests of the Quanzhen Sect.

Taoist Priests

Taoism is divided into the Quanzhen and Zhengyi sects. The Quanzhen Sect has stricter taboos and regulations, and the priests are required to live in monasteries, and forbidden to marry or to eat meat. The Zhengyi Sect stresses personal cultivation, and the priests may live at home or in monasteries, and are allowed to marry and to eat meat when it is not a fasting period.

Taoist priests of the Zhengyi Sect.

A prayer gathering on Mount Wudang.

Taoist Rituals
Each Taoist Ritual has certain procedures and
contents. During a ritual, Taoist priests and
masters all wear ceremonial dress, use various
musical instruments and ritual articles
according to the forms of the ritual, say prayers,
and summon deities and guardians.

Burning prayers.

Burning incense.

The site of a ritual.

The Opening Ceremony.

The Grand Universe Ceremony.
The Grand Universe Ceremony is held to pray for prosperity and peace in the nation, good weather for crops, and world peace. It is usually initiated by a community or several Taoist monasteries. The solemn ceremony lasts for three, five or seven days.

Chanting Prayers.

A repentance ritual with Taoist nuns.

A ritual for delivering the soul of the deceased.

入真門秉真心參遁真玄真自在

Chanting prayers and repentance.

A senior master is walking along the form of the Plough.

青玄壇

五色運花作結瓶起

Senior Master Jiang Zhilin purifying the altar.

A "Flower Scattering" ritual by Taoist nuns from Hong Kong.

Foreign Taoist priests are walking around the statues of Taoist Deities.

The ceremony to send off deities at the conclusion of the Grand Universe Ceremony.

Taoist disciples entering the altar
one after the other.

Taoist Initiation
Initiation is a solemn ritual of the Quanzhen Sect
of Taoism. A reputable priest (Master of Initiation)
teaches principles and regulations to Taoist
disciples, explains the significance of abiding by
the principles and regulations, and demonstrates
the rituals and ceremonies according to the
principles and regulations. After education and
examination, the Taoist disciples receive their
credentials, then practice self-cultivation
according to Taoist principles and seek
immortality.

Taoist disciples paying respects to the Abbot and the Eight Masters.

Initiation and credential conferment.

Performing the initiation.

Communal dining hall.

Performing the ceremony.

The eight masters officiating at the credential conferring ceremony.

Taoist disciples awaiting the Initiation Supervising Master to explain the sculpture in the Jade Emperor Hall.

The Conferment of Credentials.
The Conferment of Credentials is a solemn cerem of the Taoist Zhengyi Sect, where senior mas (Credential Conferring Masters) confer creden to Taoist disciples. Having received the credent Taoist disciples practice self-cultivation through levels of the Zhengyi Sect, redeeming others as as themselves.

The Master of Initiation officiating at an initiation ceremony.

Chanting prayers.

Listening to the explanation of the sculpture.

A prayer gathering.

Life of Taoists

Meditating on the Tao.

Playing the zither.

Playing *weiqi* or *go*.

Practicing calligraphy.

The pagoda tomb of Zang Tui, a Taoist priest said to have ascended to heaven and become immortal on Mount Wudang.

III. Taoist Musical Instruments and Ritual Articles

During various Taoist rituals, certain musical instruments and ritual articles are used. Seen most often are Taoist vestments such as the ritual robes and headdress; musical instruments such as drums, bells and chime stones; exorcism articles such as swords, seals and talismans; incense burner tables, scrolls and streamers, etc. The major ritual articles are swords, seals and talismans.

The Celestial Master's sword in and out its sheath.

The sword is also known as the Sword of the Seven Stars, as it bears the carved image of the seven stars of the Northern Dipper. Said to have magical powers of exorcism, it is one of the three treasures of Celestial Master Zhang, one of the founders of religious Taoism.

A peach-wood sword.

①

Seals and Tablets

These articles represent the authority of a deity or a celestial master. During a ritual, the Taoist priest uses them to beckon the wind or rain, summon deities and celestial generals, exorcise evil, subdue demons and monsters, and redeem the spirits of the dead.

A "mother and son" seal bearing the symbols of the Eight Immortals.
a. An aerial view of the top of the seal.
b. The seal can be disassembled into a larger ("mother") seal and a smaller ("son") one.

②

A seal with the words of Celestial Master.

A tablet bearing images of two deities on the front and the back respectively.

a. The image of Marshal Yin. b. The left side of the tablet.

c. The image of Wang Lingguan. d. The right side of the tablet.

e. The top of the tablet. f. The bottom of the tablet.

The handed down Celestial Master's house-guarding charm.
It is used to safeguard houses, exorcise evil, and subdue demons and monsters.

An initiation card of the Taoist Quanzhen Sect.

太上
津脈
龍門
正宗

A ritual table.

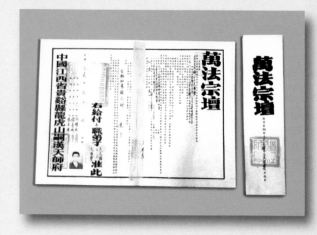

A credential of the Taoist Zhengyi Sect.

Taoist ritual rods.

Taoist documents, sculptures, jade tablet and bowl.

A drum, a repentance bell, and a gong.

A feather fan.

A chime stone, a wooden clapper, and a hand bell.

A whisk.

Taoist Vestments. ▶
Taoist priests usually wear blue or
dark blue robes (or white ones in
summer). During a ritual, they wear
different ritual robes according to the
roles they play.

A repentance robe.
This is the robe worn by a senior
master during prayer or repentance
gatherings. A purple robe is worn at
prayer rituals, while a yellow robe
is worn at soul-delivering rituals.
The robe is embroidered with
images such as dragons, tigers,
cranes and immortals.

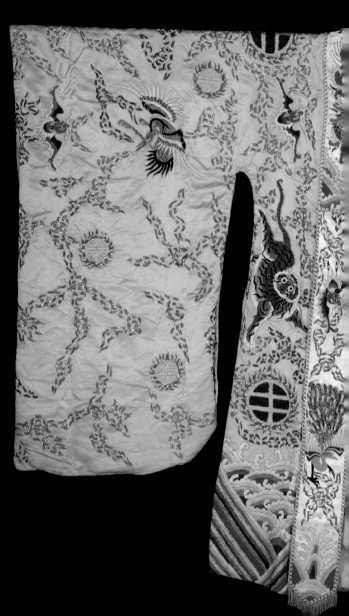

A Taoist ritual robe.
Taoists wear this style of robe at
prayer or repentance gatherings, or
at rituals.

A senior master's robe.

This is a robe worn by a senior master during rituals. Senior masters of the highest rank wear yellow robes, while other senior masters wear dark blue or red. The robe, when spread, is square in shape, symbolizing the four directions of the universe.

A netted headdress and a
gold Taoist cap.
Taoist priests wear netted
headdresses at rituals.
Senior masters wear gold
Taoist caps.

Taoist ritual boots.
Senior masters wear this
type of boots at grand
ceremonies.

A scroll and streamers bearing cloud
and dragon patterns.

IV. Taoist *Gongfu* and Alchemy

Accentuating life and abhorring death, Taoism believes that one can achieve immortality through self-cultivation. The Taoists both created and adopted many methods of self-cultivation, such as sitting motionless, concentrating of the mind, promoting the flow of *qi*, breathing, combining of controlled breathing and physical exercises, and practicing martial arts *(gongfu)*. Most traditional Chinese methods of health preservation, including *qigong*, martial arts and traditional Chinese medicine, have links with Taoism. It is said that *taijiquan* (Chinese shadow boxing) was invented by Zhang Sanfeng, a Taoist priest of Mount Wudang. Ancient Chinese Taoists were also enthusiastic alchemists, who attempted to produce immortality pills by smelting minerals such as aluminum and mercury. The experiments in alchemy, though irrational from a modern viewpoint, greatly promoted advances in science and technology in ancient China, including the production of gunpowder and ancient chemistry.

Keeping peace and tranquiliity of mind (a Taoist
gongfu of sitting still and breathing).

The magic *gongfu* of lifting oneself with two fingers (an internal exercise).

Pushing hands with empty step *(taijiquan)*.

殿皇玉

聖義咫尺天執掌陰陽生萬物

Sword-fighting on top of a mountain (swordsmanship).

An illustration of the way of self-cultivation.

The alchemical burner of Ge Hong at the ancient Chongxu Taoist Temple on Mount Luofu. ▶

An illustration of the inner channels.

◄ An alchemical burner
   on Mount Wudang.

奪得黃芽在字中　急忙切莫厭勾勾
滿身陰汞烟飛漢　一得陽鉛禽入籠
眷戀宣殊紀兒母　扣詰無異牝逢雄
精勤火候無令失
十月胎圓壽不窮

九鼎

金丹秘術起九人　六百篇將九道名
帝為範來嘗始怖　軒皇鑄鼎道方成
選時須合丹家法　用後無令厭物睚
節候換時週後始　煉成龍物自來迎

進火

太　太
簇　蔟
　　呂
　　大
　　呂
夷　　
則　鐘
　　黃
鐘　
流　
姑　
　　
呂　
仲　

抱元

朝朝金鼎飛炎烟　氣足河車運上天
甘露徧空滋萬景　靈泉一派汎長川
猶如雀卵圓圓大　閒似隨珠類類圓
龍子脫胎丹入口　此身已是陸行仙

金液

煉丹本是一年功　兩月都緣要住工
克遇上元時便止　鶴逢七月半鳥終
早鐘水潺因差過　兩順風調鳥適中
刊德既加宜沐浴　傾危斷不到吾竄

朝元

功足丹成子脫胎　且逃換面逐輪迴
色身雖已堅難壞　慧照當從定裏開
念念覺圓無一物　頭頭顯露起纏埃
九年面壁成何事　雙履振蘆任去來

還元

形神俱妙道為徒　性命雙圓合太虛
實詔降時騰鶴馭　王書拜後且充居
仙宜恒赫誰論貴　濁世煎熬且克居
積德勤求終有遇　問君何事獨躊躕

南非南芳東非東　一靈妙有素圓通
賢愚本自無分別　九聖何嘗有異同
認赤作朱成性習　呼娘為母熟摸錦
吾之真原空不實　一切卜卜

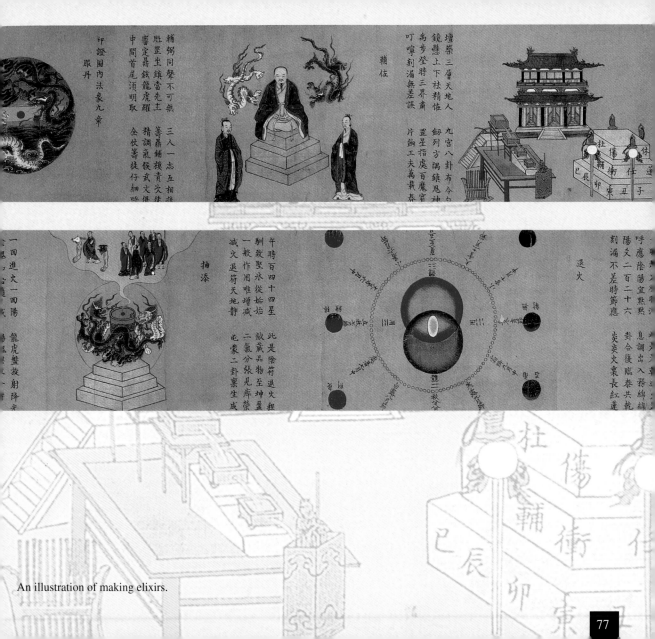

An illustration of making elixirs.

V. Sacred Mountains, Taoist Palaces and Temples

Taoists venerate sacred mountains, wherein they believe deities and immortals dwell, and which also provide tranquil environments ideal for their self-cultivation. Therefore, early Taoist priests lived on sacred mountains. Later, some Taoist priests accepted appointments at the imperial court, and lived in temples built for them, at the orders of the emperors, in cities. With the development and flourishing of Taoism, many large sites of Taoist activity were built in sacred mountains and cities, some of which are called "palaces" because of their palatial dimensions.

The Temple of Princess Aurora.

Mount Tai (in Shandong Province).
Mount Tai has been regarded as a sacred mountain from ancient times, reputed as the First Mount in the World. It is said that the Great Emperor of the Eastern Mountain, the God of Mount Tai, rules over people's life, death and fortunes; and that his daughter Princess Aurora protects women and children.

The South Gate to Heaven and the Ladder to Heaven.

The Hall of Heavenly Gifts in the Temple
to the God of Mount Tai, on Mount Tai.

Murals in the Temple to the God of
Mount Tai in Mount Tai.

The North Peak of Mount Hua.

Mount Hua (in Shaanxi Province). As a saying goes, "There is only one path up Mount Hua from ancient times." Mount Hua is known for its magnificence and steepness. The legendary Taoist Priest Chen Tuan of the 10th century lived a reclusive life here.

The gate of the Temple of Mount Hua.

The Magic Axe in Mount Hua, said to have been used by Chenxiang to cut the mountain to rescue his mother.

The Forbidden City on Mount Wudang.

The ruins of the arch gate of the Yuxu Taoist Palace on Mount Wudang.

Mount Wudang (in Hubei Province). Mount Wudang is said to be the place where the Great Emperor Zhenwu achieved Tao and ascended Heaven. It is also the place where the famous Taoist priest Zhang Sanfeng practiced self-cultivation. Wudang swordsmanship and *taijiquan* have long been famous around the country.

The Nanyan Taoist Palace on Mount Wudang.

The Dragon-head Incense Burner
on Mount Wudang.

The Golden Peak of Mount Wudang.

The snow-covered Mount Qingcheng.

Mount Qingcheng (in Sichuan Province).
This mountain was one of the major locales where Celestial Master Zhang taught the "Tao". The cave he used to stay in still exists today.

The entrance to Mount Qingcheng.

The Cave of the Celestial Master on Mount Qingcheng.

The interior of Daluosanjing
Hall in the Yangtai Taoist
Palace on Mount Wangwu.

Mount Wangwu (in Henan Province).
Known as the "First Dwelling of Immortals" among the Taoists, the mountain used to be the place where many famous Taoist priests practiced self-cultivation.

A corner of the Yuhuang Pavilion in the Yangtai Taoist Palace on Mount Wangwu.

Mount Kongdong (in Gansu Province).
Legend recounts that the Yellow Emperor
used to ask the Immortal Guangchengzi
about Tao.

Waves of clouds on Mount Kongdong.

The Incense-burner Monastery on White Cloud Mountain.

White Cloud Mountain (in Shaanxi Province).
This mountain boasts the largest Taoist monastery
complex in northwest China.

Zhenwu Hall on White Cloud Mountain.

Layout of the Louguan Terrace on Mount Zhongnan

1 Furnace for making pills of immortality
2 Immortals-gathering Pavilion
3 Huaisu Pavilion
4 Pavilion for Welcoming the Sun
5 Scripture-chanting Terrace
6 Pagoda of Mantle and Alms Bowl
7 Zongshen Taoist Palace
8 Conglin House
9 Girl Spring
10 Ancient Pagoda
11 Tomb of Lao Zi
12 Pavilion of Listening to the Immortals
13 Cave of Master Lü
14 Pavilion of Theophany

The Chongyang Taoist Palace in Shaanxi Province got its name because Wang Chongyang, the founder of the Taoist Quanzhen Sect, used to practice self-cultivation here.

Mount Zhongnan (in Shaanxi Province).
It is said that, during the Zhou Dynasty, Yin Xi, head of Hangu Pass, used to observe the stars and the air from a thatched house that he built on the mountain. One day he saw a mass of purple air coming from the east, and knew that a sage was crossing the pass. He then waited until he met Lao Zi. There still exists the Sculpture-Exposition Terrace, where Lao Zi once taught Yin Xi the *Dao De Jing*.

Laojun Hall in the Louguan Terrace on Mount Zhongnan.

雙龍衛乾坤

八卦涵宇宙

The Eight-Diagram Gate of Lingzhi Garden at the Celestial Master's Residence on Dragon and Tiger Mountain, Jiangxi Province. The descendents of Celestial Master Zhang Daoling inherited his title and lived in the Celestial Master's Residence.

The Ordination Altar at the White Cloud Temple.

A decorated archway.

The White Cloud Temple (in Beijing).
The White Cloud Temple in Beijing was first built in the Tang Dynasty. Beginning with Qiu Chuji of the Yuan Dynasty, all the heads of the Quanzhen Sect have lived here, and as a result the temple became much better known. Today it houses the office of the Taoist Association of China.

Wofeng Bridge and Lingguan Hall.

North

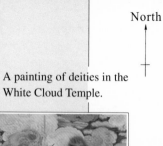

A painting of deities in the
White Cloud Temple.

Layout of the White Cloud Temple in Beijing

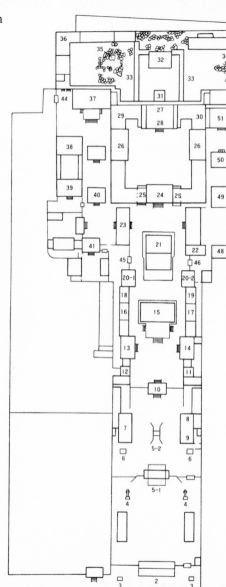

33 Long corridor
34 Friendly Crane Pavilion
35 Hall of Fragrance
36 Retreat Tower
37 Yuanchen Hall
38 Hall of Master L
39 Hall of Eight Immortals
40 Yuanjun Hall
41 Memorial Hall
42 Kitchen
43 Fasting room
44 Rear gate
45 Tufu Taoist Palace
46 Doufu Taoist Palace
47 Pagoda of Master Luo
48 Hall of Three Stars
48 Hall of Journey of Salvation
50 Zhenwu Hall
51 Leizu Hall

1 Screen wall
2 Decorated archway
3 Lions
4 Ornamental columns
5-1 Front Gate
5-2 Wofeng Bridge
6 Mast
7 Shifang Hall
8 Reception room
9 Cloud and Water Hall
10 Lingguan Hall
11 Bell tower
12 Drum tower
13 Hall of the God of Wealth
14 Hall of Three Gods
15 Hall of the Jade Emperor
16 Hall of Cleaning
17 Xiuzhen Hall
18 Hall of Diligence and Peace
19 Yangzhen Hall
20-1 Hall of the Medicine King
20-2 Hall of Rescuing the Suffered
21 Hall of Seven True Saints
22 Hall of Merit and Virtue
23 Duty room
24 Hall of Master Qiu
25 Second gate
26 Halls for accommodating visiting guests
27 Three Purities Tower
28 Hall of Four Guardians
29 Chaotian Tower
30 Scripture Tower
31 Ordination Altar
32 Could-assembling House

青羊宮

The Black Goat Taoist Palace in Chengdu.

As legend recounts, Lao Zi parted with Yin Xi at Hangu Pass, saying he would be reborn at the market selling black goats three years later. Yin Xi arrived in Chengdu at the said time, and followed a boy leading a black goat to his home, where, as expected, he witnessed that Lao Zi was reborn. People of later generations built the Black Goat Taoist Palace to commemorate this story.

The Eight-trigram Pavilion at the Black Goat Taoist Palace.

The Baopu Temple in Hangzhou. It is said that Ge Hong (also known as Baopuzi), a well-known Taoist priest of the Jin Dynasty, used to make immortality pills here.

The Eight Immortals Taoist Palace in Xi'an.
As legend has it, this used to be a wine shop in Chang'an (today's Xi'an) during the Tang Dynasty, where the Immortal Lü Dongbin met Zhong Liquan and achieved Tao.

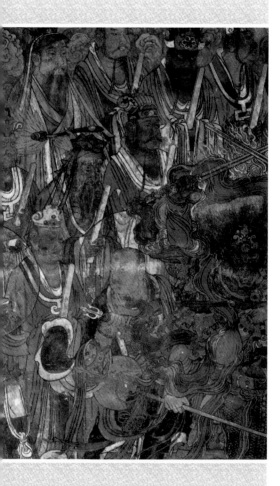

A disc-shaped caisson ceiling in the Hall of the Three Purities at the Yongle Taoist Palace in Ruicheng, Shanxi Province. ▼

◀ "Worshiping Heaven," a mural in the Yongle Taoist Palace in Shanxi Province.

The Taoist murals in Yongle Palace are the largest in scale and best preserved of their kind in China today.

The Mazu Temple in Macao.

The Temple of the God of the Town in Shanghai.

The Laojuntai Temple of the Quanzhen Sect in the Ningxia Hui Autonomous Region.

The Fung Ying Seen Koon in Hong Kong.

The Zhinan Taoist Palace in Taipei.

Sketch Map of Sacred Taoist Mountains, Palaces and Temples in China

1 White Cloud Temple in Beijing
2 Supreme Purity Taoist Palace in Shenyang
3 Qianshan Mountain in Anshan, Liaoning Province
4 Mount Tai in Taian, Shandong Province
5 Eight Immortals Taoist Palace in Xi'an
6 Mount Hua in Huayin County, Shaanxi Province
7 White Cloud Mountain in Jiaxian County, Shaanxi Province
8 Chongyang Taoist Palace in Huxian County, Shaanxi Province
9 Mount Zhongnan in Zhouzhi County, Shaanxi Province
10 Songshan Mountain in Dengfeng County, Henan Province
11 Supreme Purity Taoist Palace in Luyi County, Henan Province
12 Qiyun Mountain in Xiuning County, Anhui Province
13 Maoshan Mountain in Jurong County, Jiangsu Province
14 Xuanmiao Temple in Suzhou
15 Temple of the God of the Town in Shanghai
16 The Black Goat Taoist Palace in Chengdu
17 Mount Qingcheng in Dujiangyan, Sichuan Province
18 Laojun Cave in Chongqing
19 Changchun Temple in Wuhan
20 Mountain Wudang in Danjiangkou, Hubei Province
21 Hengshan Mountain in Hengyang, Hunan Province
22 Mount Lushan in Jiujiang, Jiangxi Province
23 Dragon and Tiger Mountain in Yingtan, Jiangxi Province
24 Baopu Temple in Hangzhou
25 Wuyi Mountain in Fujian Province
26 Sanyuan Taoist Palace in Guangzhou
27 Mount Luofu in Boluo County, Guangdong Province
28 Immortals Cave in Guiyang
29 Weibao Mountain in Weishan County, Yunnan Province
30 White Cloud Temple in Lanzhou
31 Mount Kongdong in Pingliang, Gansu Province
32 Laojuntai Temple of the Quanzhen Sect in Zhongwei County, Ningxia Hui Autonomous Region
33 Tulou Temple in Xining

34 Supreme Purity Taoist Palace in Huhhot, Inner Mongol Autonomous Region
35 Fushou Taoist Palace in Liaoyuan, Jilin Province
36 Tianxian Taoist Palace in Mudanjiang, Heilongjiang Province
37 Yongle Taoist Palace in Reicheng, Shanxi Province
38 Laoshan Mountain in Qingdao
39 Hengshan Mountain in Hunyuan County, Shanxi Province
40 Wanshou Taoist Palace in the Western Hills in Xinjian County, Jiangxi Province
41 Mount Wangwu in Jiyuan, Henan Province
42 Zhinan Taoist Palace in Taipei

Main Taoist Festivals and Grand Ceremonies

Taoist Festival	Lunar Date	Taoist Ceremony
Birthday of Jade Emperor	9th of the first month	Grand Ceremony for Blessings
Lantern Festival	15th of the first month	Grand Ceremony for Blessings
Birthday of Master Qiu	19th of the first month	Grand Ceremony for Blessings
Supreme Purity Festival	15th of the second month	Grand Ceremony for Blessings
Qingming Festival	4th or 5th of the fourth month	Grand Ceremony for the Deceased
Birthday of Master Lü	14th of the fourth month	Grand Ceremony for Blessings
Lofty Purity Festival	Summer Solstice	Grand Ceremony for Blessings
Zhongyuan Festival	15th of the seventh month	Grand Ceremonies for Blessings during the Day and for the Deceased at Night
Nine-Emperor Festival	9th of the ninth month	Grand Ceremony for Blessings
Minsuila Festival	1st of the tenth month	Grand Ceremony for the Deceased
Xiayuan Festival	15th of the tenth month	Grand Ceremony for Blessings
Precious Purity Festival	Winter Solstice	Grand Ceremony for Blessings

图书在版编目（CIP）数据

中国道教／中国道教协会主编. －北京：外文出版社，2002.7
（中华风物）

ISBN 7-119-03061-2

Ⅰ.中… Ⅱ.中… Ⅲ.道教－简介－中国－英文 Ⅳ.B95

中国版本图书馆 CIP 数据核字(2002)第 026217 号

"中华风物"编辑委员会

总 顾 问：叶小文　闵智亭
顾 问：张继禹　袁炳栋　陈红星
主 编：肖晓明
编 委：肖晓明　李振国　田　辉　呼宝珉
　　　　房永明　胡开敏　崔黎丽　兰佩瑾

责任编辑：胡开敏
撰 文：尹志华
英文翻译：张韶宁　陈海燕
英文审定：王增芬
内文设计：席恒青
封面设计：蔡　荣

（本书部分图片得到中国建筑工业出版社、
光复书局、台北蓬一玄道长等相助，特此
鸣谢。）

中 国 道 教

中国道教协会 编

ⓒ 外文出版社

外文出版社出版
（中国北京百万庄大街24号）
邮政编码：100037
外文出版社网址：http://www.flp.com.cn
外文出版社电子邮件地址：info@flp.com.cn
　　　　　　　　　　 sales@flp.com.cn
外文出版社照排中心制作
天时印刷(深圳)有限公司印刷
中国国际图书贸易总公司发行
（中国北京车公庄西路35号）
北京邮政信箱第399号　邮政编码　100044
2002年(24开)第1版
2002年第1版第1次印刷
（英）
ISBN 7-119-03061-2/J·1592（外）
05800（平）
85-E-537P

Post Card

FOREIGN LANGUAGES PRESS · 外 文 出 版 社

A senior master purifying the altar